D0821782

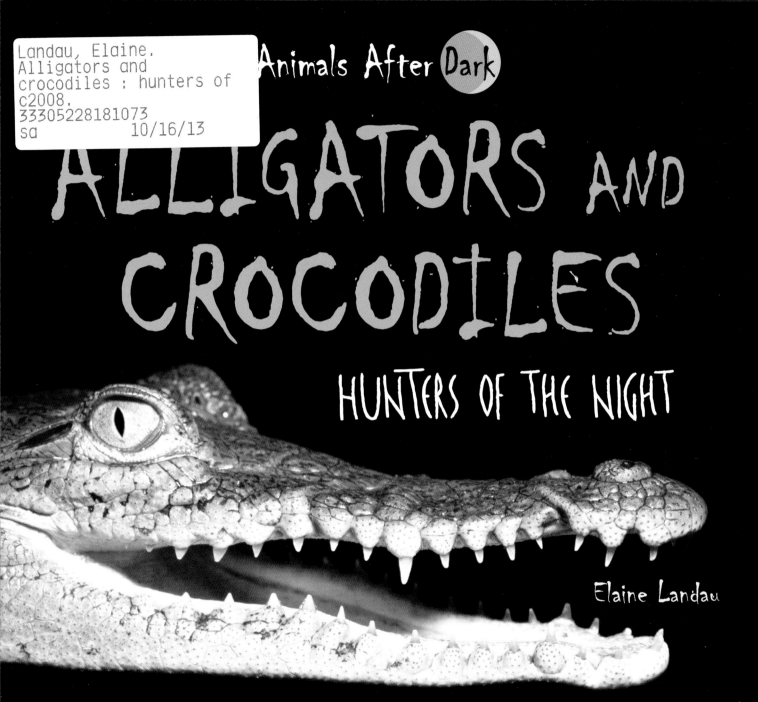

Landau, Elaine.
Alligators and
crocodiles : hunters of
c2008.
33305228181073
sa   10/16/13

Animals After **Dark**

ALLIGATORS AND CROCODILES

HUNTERS OF THE NIGHT

Elaine Landau

WORDS TO KNOW

crocodilians (CROC-oh-dill-yans)— The reptile group that crocodiles and alligators belong to.

prey—An animal hunted by another animal for food.

endangered—In danger of dying out.

reptiles—Animals that have backbones and lungs and are usually covered with scales. Also, their body temperature adjusts to the area they are in.

marshes—Swampy wetlands.

predator—An animal that hunts other animals for food.

species—A type of animal.

CONTENTS

A crocodile opens its mouth to attack.

AFTER DARK

It is a hot summer night. An ox is drinking from a river. The river is silent. Yet a hungry crocodile is quietly swimming toward the ox.

Seconds later, the crocodile grabs the ox in its jaws. The ox is pulled into the water. It tries to fight back but cannot. The crocodile quickly drags the ox beneath the water. The ox soon drowns.

The crocodile now will eat until it is full. This crocodile will not be hungry for days.

A LOOK AT ALLIGATORS AND CROCODILES

You can learn a lot from an animal's skull. A crocodile (left) has a thinner head than an alligator (right).

Most crocodiles and alligators are large. The American alligator grows to about eight to ten feet but can be as long as nineteen feet.

There are fourteen different species, or types, of crocodiles. Most adult crocodiles are about eight to twelve feet long. Some Australian saltwater crocodiles have grown to more than twenty feet. That is about as long as a bus.

Crocodiles and alligators both have rough, scaly skin. There are bony plates on their backs and smaller ones on their bellies.

Yet there are differences between these animals too. A crocodile has a narrow V-shaped head. An alligator's head is wider and rounder. It is shaped like a U.

Both alligators and crocodiles have sharp, pointed teeth. The teeth on a crocodile's lower jaw show when its mouth is closed.

Crocodiles are more likely to attack than alligators.

Alligators and crocodiles are reptiles. Their body temperature does not stay the same. It changes to match the area they are in. On cool mornings, they often rest in the sun. This heats them up. When it gets too hot, they cool off in the water.

Crocodiles and alligators are good swimmers. Their long, slim bodies move well in the water. They use their strong tails as paddles to push them along. Sometimes they will lash out at an enemy with their tails.

Crocodiles are
great swimmers.

DINOSAUR RELATIVES

Crocodiles and alligators are crocodilians (CROC-oh-dill-yans). Crocodilians are a group of reptiles. Some species of crocodilians lived more than 200 million years ago. They were here when huge dinosaurs roamed Earth.

Back then, a few crocodilians were as big as dinosaurs. Among the largest of these was *Sarcosuchus* (SAR-co-suk-us) *imperator* or "flesh crocodile emperor." This crocodilian was forty feet long. It weighed ten tons—about as much as forty adult male gorillas. Sarcosuchus is also called "SuperCroc."

Like the dinosaurs, the SuperCroc died out.

A scientist stands by the skull of the SuperCroc. It had six-foot-long jaws and more than one hundred teeth!

MADE FOR NIGHT LIFE

You can see crocodiles and alligators during the day. They often rest in the sun. But they move around more at night.

Crocodiles and alligators see well in the dark. They can spot prey that might not see them. They can also smell and hear nearby animals after dark. These reptiles do not need daylight to find a meal.

This alligator searches for food at night.

Only this alligator's eyes
and nostrils can be seen.

HUNTING AND EATING

Crocodiles and alligators often sneak up on their prey. It is hard to see these reptiles in the water. Sometimes they look like floating logs. Other times, only their eyes and **nostrils**, or nose openings, show.

Crocodiles and alligators use their powerful jaws to grab their prey. They usually drag the animal to the water. Crocodiles and alligators do not chew their food. They swallow small prey whole. These meals go down in one gulp.

Eating larger prey takes more work. Crocodiles and alligators twist and pull their prey's body until smaller chunks break off. These pieces are swallowed in one gulp as well. Crocodiles and alligators throw back their heads while swallowing. This makes the food fall down their throats.

Crocodiles and alligators are meat eaters. Smaller alligators and crocodiles usually eat fish, turtles, birds, and frogs. Bigger ones eat monkeys, oxen, pigs, deer, antelope, and other large animals.

A crocodile throws back its head to swallow some food.

17

HOME SWEET HOME

Crocodiles and alligators live in places where the weather is warm. This is especially true of crocodiles. They are in the hottest parts of Africa, Australia, Southeast Asia, and North and South America.

American alligators mostly live in the southeastern United States. They are in Alabama, Arkansas, North and South Carolina, Florida, Georgia, Louisiana, Mississippi, Oklahoma, and Texas.

Alligators live in fresh water. They are found in swamps, marshes, ponds, lakes, canals, and some rivers.

Some species of crocodiles live in salty waters near the ocean. There are also freshwater crocodiles. These are found in swamps, lakes, and other freshwater spots. Other crocodiles live in both salt water and fresh water.

This alligator lives in a swamp.

Baby alligators can be easily eaten by other animals because they are so small and cannot fight back as well as adult alligators.

STAYING ALIVE

Adult crocodiles and alligators do not have many predators. Few other animals are as large and strong. However, large snakes in Asia have attacked crocodiles. Lately, big snakes have attacked alligators in Florida.

Crocodiles and alligators have also been killed while hunting. Crocodiles sometimes attack the babies of big animals like elephants. If the mothers of these animals are nearby, they defend their babies. Crocodiles have died in these fights.

Very young crocodiles and alligators cannot defend themselves. Snakes, raccoons, turtles, owls, and other animals eat them. Large crocodiles and alligators sometimes eat smaller ones as well.

An alligator moves eggs around her nest with her mouth.

MATING AND RAISING BABIES

Crocodiles and alligators mate with members of their own species to have babies. After mating, the female builds a nest.

Some female crocodiles dig a hole in the sand. They lay their eggs there. Then they cover the eggs with sand. These make little hills, or mounds. Others build mound nests of soil, leaves, and twigs. Female alligators build mound nests, too.

The female lays her eggs in the center of the mound. Then she covers her eggs. She stays close by to guard the nest.

Female crocodiles and alligators stay with their babies for about two years. They carry them to the water in their mouths. They also try to protect them from predators.

Two scientists check to see
if an alligator is healthy.
Only adult scientists should
get close to an alligator.

ALLIGATORS, CROCODILES, AND PEOPLE

In the past, crocodiles and alligators were hunted for their skins. Handbags, belts, and shoes were often made from them and sold.

Many crocodiles and alligators also died off when swamps and wetlands were drained to build farms and towns. Boats scared them away from their nesting areas, too. Each year many eggs were destroyed or could not hatch.

Over time, some species of crocodiles and alligators became endangered, or in danger of dying out. Nations passed laws to protect these animals. Before long, the numbers of crocodiles and alligators began to rise.

STAYING SAFE

Now, in some areas, humans live fairly close to alligators and crocodiles. These animals do not usually look for people to attack. They have a natural fear of humans. It is best to keep it that way since they sometimes do attack if people get too close. If you live or visit where there are crocodiles or alligators, follow these tips:

- Stay away from crocodiles or alligators.

- Never throw anything at these reptiles or tease them.

- Do not feed these animals. It makes them lose their fear of humans.

- Do not swim where you know there are crocodiles or alligators.

- Crocodiles and alligators are wild animals. They can never be pets.

Crocodiles and alligators attack quickly. People should not get close to them.

This dwarf crocodile lives in Africa. It is smaller than other crocodiles.

FUN FACTS ABOUT ALLIGATORS AND CROCODILES

★ Ancient crocodile mummies have been found in Egypt.

★ The American alligator can stay underwater for up to two hours.

★ Crocodiles and alligators keep growing all their lives.

★ Crocodiles can go for months without eating. They live on the fat stored in their tails.

★ Crocodiles and alligators never run out of teeth. New teeth grow to replace those that fall out.

TO KNOW MORE ABOUT ALLIGATORS AND CROCODILES

BOOKS:

Murray, Julie. *Crocodiles*. Edina, Minn.: ABDO Publishing, 2005.

Royston, Angela. *Alligators and Crocodiles*. Mankato, Minn.: Weigl Publishers, 2003.

Stone, Tanya Lee. *Crocodilians*. San Diego, Ca: Blackbirch Press, 2003.

Whitehouse, Patricia. *Alligator*. Chicago, Ill.: Heinemann Library, 2003.

INTERNET ADDRESSES:

Alligators: Everglades National Park

<http://www.nps.gov/ever/ naturescience/alligatorindepth.htm>

All you ever need to know about alligators!

Crocodiles!—A PBS Web site

<http://www.pbs.org/wgbh/nova/ teacher/activities/2509_crocs.html/>

You will find lots of fun facts about crocodiles here. Do not miss the Clickable Croc link for some great close-up science.

INDEX

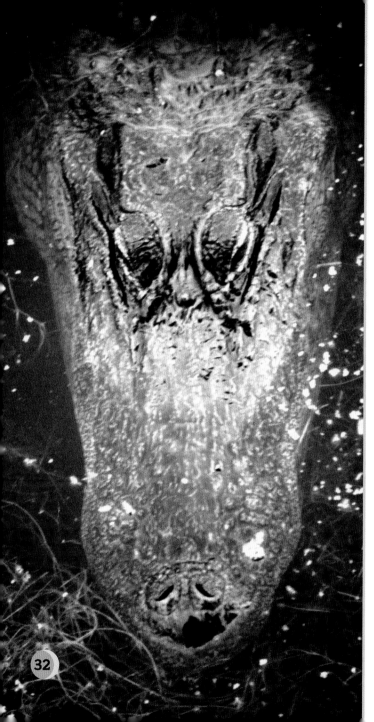

Enslow Elementary, an imprint of Enslow Publishers, Inc.

Enslow Elementary® is a registered trademark of Enslow Publishers, Inc.

Copyright © 2008 by Elaine Landau

All rights reserved.

No part of this book may be reproduced by any means without the written permission of the publisher.

Library of Congress Cataloging-in-Publication Data

Landau, Elaine.
    Alligators and crocodiles : hunters of the night / Elaine Landau.
       p. cm. — (Animals after dark)
    Includes bibliographical references and index.
    ISBN-13: 978-0-7660-2771-8
    ISBN-10: 0-7660-2771-6
    1. Alligators—Juvenile literature. 2. Crocodiles—Juvenile literature. I. Title.
QL666.C925L345 2008
597.98—dc22   2006034066

Printed in the United States of America
072012 Lake Book Manufacturing, Inc., Melrose Park, IL

10 9 8 7 6 5 4 3

To Our Readers: We have done our best to make sure all Internet Addresses in this book were active and appropriate when we went to press. However, the author and the publisher have no control over and assume no liability for the material available on those Internet sites or on other Web sites they may link to. Any comments or suggestions can be sent by e-mail to comments@enslow.com or to the address on the back cover.

Series Literacy Advisor: Dr. Allan A. De Fina, Department of Literacy Education, New Jersey City University.

Illustration Credits: Chris Johns/Getty Images, pp. 22–23; Farrell Grehan/Getty Images, pp. 20–21; Fritz Polking/Visuals Unlimited, pp. 12–13; Hollingsworth, John and Karen/U.S. Fish and Wildlife Refuge, pp. 24–25; Jack Milchanowski/Visuals Unlimited , pp. 4–5; Jeff Rotman/Alamy, pp. 8–9; Joe McDonald/Visuals Unlimited, p. 6; © 2006 Jupiterimages Corporation, pp. 2 (right), 3, 14–15, 29 (right), 32; Ken Lucas/Visuals Unlimited, p. 28; Lee Prince/Shutterstock, pp. 2 (left), 18–19; Manoj Shah/Getty images, pp. 16–17; Mike Hettwer, National Geographic, p. 11; Stuart Dee/Getty Images, p. 27; Tom Antos, p. 29 (left).

Cover Illustration: Kevin Schafer/Getty Images (front and back cover).

Enslow Elementary
an imprint of

 Enslow Publishers, Inc.
40 Industrial Road
Box 398
Berkeley Heights, NJ 07922
USA

http://www.enslow.com